C000025490

THIS NOTEBOOK

BELONGS TO :

Printed in Great Britain
by Amazon

72388449R00072